ADAMS

THE FIRST ADAM & THE LAST ADAM

ALFRED BETHEL

ISBN: 9798358210370

DEDICATION

This book is dedicated to Jesus Christ our Lord. In whom we have redemption through his blood, the forgiveness of sins according to the riches of his grace. In him we also, when we heard the word of truth, the gospel of our salvation, and believed in him, were sealed with the promised Holy Spirit. So that through the Holy Spirit, our whole spirit, soul and body will be kept blameless at the coming of our Lord Jesus Christ.

CONTENTS

ACKNOWLEDGMENTS

First and foremost, I sincerely appreciate the Lord Jesus Christ for his revelation and enlightenment that inspired the writing of this book. My profound acknowledgement also goes to the writings of the great minister of God Waterman Nee, which were instructive in this project. I cannot but appreciate my family and friends that contributed in one way or the other to the success of this book. I specially recognize Temitope Dada, Goodluck Eka Etoh and my very wonderful brother Kayode Olatunji.

Thank you all.

I love you all.

1 ENCOUNTER WITH THE FIRST MAN

As in His father's house are many mansions, even so on the Christian journey are many sojourners. Some seem to be struggling with this Christ-life, some other seem to be stable with it, while some other seem to have entered into perfection. One would have thought Alice was of the last category, with her reaction to the recent scandal in the fellowship.

In a Community largely populated by Students of institutions of higher learning and graduates who were still pretty much single, was the Rose of Sharon Fellowship (RSF), a youth Christian fellowship commissioned by the Holy Spirit, established based on the truth, life and spirit of God's word and on sound biblical doctrines and beliefs. RSF since inception was reputed to preach the true gospel of Christ with the demonstration of the spirit and power, and as such, a lot of youth and teenagers found it—the best place to truly worship and serve God.

Everything seemed to be going well in the fellowship until some dirty secrets came into the open, and that reached its height when two members of the fellowship executives were caught with their hands in the cookie jar.

Of course, that called for an immediate disciplinary action and the two sisters that were involved were summoned to a meeting of the executive disciplinary committee of the fellowship. Pastor Beloved in his late twenties, was the fellowship president and the chairman of the disciplinary committee. Other members of the committee were: Thomas—the brothers' coordinator, Alice—the sisters' coordinator, Julian and Sarah all in their mid-twenties.

The meeting was scheduled for 5pm but Alice got to the premise at exactly

3:50pm, she obviously could not wait to see the meeting held. And with her stern look, she appeared mostly disappointed about the recent events in the fellowship. She sat at the balcony right at the entrance of the fellowship premise, waiting for others to come as she kept herself busy with a notebook in her hand—a note where she jotted some salient points she planned to mention during the meeting.

Julian who held the key to the premise arrived exactly 4:30pm. After an usually casual exchange of pleasantries with Alice, he opened the premise and they both entered and got the premise set for the meeting. Not quite long, Sarah and Thomas joined them and they made a sitting arrangements that had two isolated seats directly facing the seats of the committee.

They began to get worried at 4:50pm that the president was not forthcoming and unreachable and just then, Janet entered. She looked guilty, shameful and sober. Definitely, she was one of the culprits. They ordered her to sit on one of the two isolated seats facing the committee seats and she did reluctantly and ashamedly.

At exactly 5:00pm, the committee members took their seats whispering to one another about the lateness of the president.

"Where is Debbie?" a question by Alice to the whole house.

"I was about to ask of her too." replied Julian directing his gaze at Janet who quickly avoided eye contact.

Just then, Sarah deemed it fit to inform them, "well... I called her phone several times a couple of hour ago but she wasn't picking her calls and the last time I tried, it was switched off. She might be avoiding us."

"Does that mean she won't be present for this meeting?" asked Alice with so much curiosity.

Thomas interjected, "Most likely. Because she already left all our social media groups and pages."

"Really?" Few of them exclaimed.

Thomas continued, "not only that, she has submitted all the fellowship items and properties in her care. In fact, she did that through courier service." The other committee members could not keep to themselves how much of a disappointment and surprise that piece of information was to them.

"Maybe we are too harsh in handling the matter," whispered Julian to the committee members in such a manner that Janet could not have heard.

Whilst others only limited their views of that Julian's opinion to mere reactions, Alice could not but speak out tough, "Did you say too harsh? Are we supposed to condone such a heinous and tarnishing scandal? For God's sake, it is so shameful and disappointing that Janet right here the fellowship vice-president and Debbie the fellowship prayer coordinator carried the precious life of God in them to do the most unspeakable, reprobate and inordinate thing. What a vile affection! Common guys! These ladies are a disgrace to redemption. With all the truths and the whole counsel of God that are being communicated in this fellowship, coupled with their own in-depth knowledge of the truth, how could they go ahead despising the cross and engage in...O God! I can't even say it."

Alice outburst occasioned a dead silence for a while and that was interrupted by their greetings to Pastor Beloved who came in with quite a heavy spirit. With his look, his heart was really burdened. He neither responded to the greetings nor said anything after taking his seat. He was seriously unhappy at the events that necessitated the meeting and so remained quiet.

Alice was not going to have another phase of dead silence, so she started the meeting, "You're welcome Mr. President! Frankly speaking, I'm quite disappointed and at the same time sorrowful about what Janet and Debbie were caught in. For Christ sake, they are both born again Christians and leaders in this fellowship. How could they go and secretly do such an ungodly thing that is scripturally condemned and even condemned largely by the world as a moral wrong?"

She turned to Janet and continued, "What happened to your salvation? What happened to your Calvary experience? You can't even have any excuse as 2 Corinthians 5:17 says 'if any man be in Christ he's a new creature, old things are passed away, behold all things are become new'. How would your own new creature still do old things? Galatians 5:24 'And they that are Christ's have crucified the flesh with the affections and lusts.' Why did you that you're of Christ still show forth lusts of the flesh? And Romans 6:6-7 says 'knowing this, that our old man is crucified with him, that the body of sin might be destroyed, that henceforth we should not serve sin. For he that is dead is freed from sin.' Janet how could you still live in sin?"

Other committee members were silent including the president. It was as if they left Alice to preside over the meeting. Janet was already in uncontrollable tears as she received those strokes of rebuke from Alice. Alice's seeming personal concern and harsh reaction about the matter could partly be understood, she was the sisters' coordinator and the culprits were sisters.

Fortunately, Julian who had been fighting back a cough lost his resisting power and surprisingly, that cough called Alice into order as she realized that she's been talking alone. "What's going on? you are all quiet, making it look as if I'm the only bad one here who is not radical enough to welcome this new development" she said, with a view to inciting them to talk.

And that worked. Thomas, Julian and Sarah quickly refuted the insinuation that they embraced the scandal. And Thomas added, "Just that, I'd rather we went right into the disciplinary measures to be taking against them."

"And since Debbie has already excommunicated herself, I will suggest we leave her out of this." remarked Sarah.

Alice who was still implacable confronted the president "And Pastor Beloved too, you're not saying anything. Remember just last month we lost a fervent brother who died of a sexually transmitted disease. Just then we got to discover that, that our born again and spirit filled brother had been sleeping with prostitutes with the life of God in him OMG! And now Janet your assistant, a respectable fellowship vice-president and Debbie, fellowship prayer coordinator were caught in such an irritable act. And we are gathered here keeping mute as if all is still well."

The president was so overwhelmed by the burden of his heart that he couldn't continue with the meeting "I'm sorry brethren, I can't continue with this meeting, kindly excuse me," he said as he walked out of the meeting.

Sarah exclaimed, "what?"

Thomas and Julian stood and ran after the president to find out what was wrong with him. Alice couldn't believe what just happened so she voiced out as usual "Pastor Beloved! are you not going to say something? Are we not supposed to talk about their suspension or something? You just walked out of the meeting like that?"

Sarah who believed that the meeting was clearly over asked Janet to take her leave and Janet did immediately. "As far as I am concerned, we need to find out what's wrong with Pastor Beloved first, is it still this issue or some other one?" said Sarah.

Alice is left alone inside the fellowship building, she couldn't help but think loud "Lord God! have mercy on us in this fellowship, these people are making it seem as if the things that are being taught here are cunningly devised fables. The gate of hell must not prevail over this fellowship." She was quiet for a while as though meditating and thereafter uttered, "Now I realize there's an emergency in the spirit and I need to gather men who have not bowed down before the altars of Baal to raise an altar of intercessory prayer for the fellowship."

For weeks, no one knew the reason behind the president's reaction and no such disciplinary meeting was called again. But the president wrote a letter to the fellowship executives to carry on with the affairs of the fellowship, for he would be away for a while. In the meantime, the disciplinary committee asked Janet to step down from her executive position and roles and join the congregation.

Pastor Beloved had locked himself in his room for about forty days, seeking the face of God concerning the burden of his heart. He knelt at his study chair and on his study table were his multi-version bible, a computer tablet, a notebook and several Christian books by classical authors. He has been doing very serious studies. He cried on his knees, "Lord! For forty days I have fasted, seeking your face, that you might enlighten my eyes of understanding on this happenings. I may be silent before men, but between you and I you know Lord, that there are thousands of questions running in my mind and I will not be silent before you my God".

And with so much tears he continues, "How come a born again and spirit filled Christians indulge in sin again and still conceive iniquity in their heart? How could Janet and Debbie who have been born of the spirit and manifested many gifts of the spirit at sundry times still do such unspeakable thing? Something is wrong somewhere that I do not know, please Lord, show me this great and mighty thing I do not know."

He began to speak in an unknown tongue as he put his head on the chair.

Six hours later, the atmosphere of the room became very tensed and extremely cold. Beloved began to feel shivery beyond his control, he felt his head was becoming distended with the overwhelming atmosphere. A Celestial Being has just appeared in his room without his knowledge because in all that, he still kept his head down on the chair praying.

The Celestial Being began to make utterances, "And the Lord God formed man of the dust of the ground, and breathed into his nostrils the breath of life; and man became a living soul. So, the first man Adam was made a living soul; while the last Adam was made a quickening spirit; But it is not the spiritual that is first but the natural, and then the spiritual; The first man was from the earth, a man of dust; the second man is from heaven; Therefore, as in Adam all die, even so in Christ shall all be made alive."

Suddenly, Beloved became conscious of the presence of the Celestial Being, "Jesus!!!" he shouted with shock after raising up his head and saw the Celestial Being.

"No, not Jesus" the Celestial Being replied.

Beloved couldn't help but ask immediately, "who are you?"

"I am the first man ADAM." replied the Celestial Being.

Beloved who hasn't gotten out of the shock of having a strange being before him continued questioning, "First man Adam... Adam as in Adam and Eve?"

The Celestial Being replied in the affirmative with a beautiful smile.

"O my God! The first one in the garden of Eden?" Beloved asked to confirm it was the same Adam he knew.

But the Celestial Being shaking his head said, "No. I am not the first one in the garden of Eden. There was an old inhabitant of the garden before my creation, he was called the ANOINTED CHERUB! Lucifer!"

"That's Ezekiel 28 verse 13 to 14." said Beloved as he recollected the scripture that establishes that.

"You are right Beloved" the Celestial Being replied. "So, I am not the first inhabitant of the garden of Eden, but I am the first man in the garden of Eden. I am man and I want to show you all of me. Rise!" Beloved stood to his feet and the Celestial Being pointed at a distance, "Take a look, what can you see?"

"I can see a building." replied Beloved as his spiritual eyes were opened.

The Celestial Being remarked, "You have seen correctly. That is my house. Come with me Beloved, let me show you this edifice."

Immediately, they were caught away as by a wind.

.

2 THE ANATOMY OF MAN

Beloved and the Celestial Being appeared at a place out of this earth, a place that can best be described as heavenly. They landed on a surface that looked like a road with a glass-like texture and they began to walk up the road.

The Celestial Being began. "Beloved! Before we get to my house, let me remind you of how I came to be. Remember after the Almighty God has created some creatures for five days, there was no man to till the ground?"

"Yes! Genesis 2 verse 5" Beloved replied confidently.

"You're right Beloved, "the Celestial Being remarked. "So the Lord God formed me (man) of the dust of the ground. And having formed me man of the dust of the ground, that which was formed was a body—a body that was lifeless and motionless. In such useless state, the man's body could not fulfil the purposes of God because it was lifeless. Then to make it function, the body needed life and so God gave man a spirit because it is the spirit that gives life. And God did this by breathing the breath of life into the nostrils of this lifeless body, and as such, a spirit from God entered into man's body."

At that point of their journey, an effigy at the top of the road came into sight.

"And as soon as the spirit came in contact with man's body, there was a reaction that produced an entity called 'Soul'. Therefore, man became a living soul." the Celestial Being added.

"O! I see," muttered Beloved who could relate with the exegesis. "But why was the entity called 'Soul' necessary?" he asked.

"We are already in my house. Let's see what we have here" responded the Celestial Being as they finally approached the effigy.

There was a fence-like cloud before the effigy. The Celestial Being held Beloved hand as they dissolved into the cloud and later appeared inside the effigy. There were three entities inside the effigy. One had the description 'Body', the second had the description 'Soul' while the third had the description 'Spirit'.

And the Celestial Being began, "Beloved! Welcome to my house called 'MAN'. I, man is made up of spirit, soul and body. And by now you should understand how these three entities came together and became man."

Beloved answered, "Yes I do. But I have a perplexity in my heart. Since the Almighty God in whose image man was made does not have body according to John 4:24, how come He made man into a body?"

The Celestial Being responded, "Beloved! The purpose for which God created man required that man should have a body. You'd find in the book of Genesis 1 verse 28 that Man was created to replenish the earth, and subdue it: and have dominion over the fish of the sea, and over the fowl of the air, and over every living thing that moves upon the earth. That meant man's sphere of influence was the earth realm, man was to interact with the earth realm. And by the nature of earth realm, no entity can function on earth without a body; so man needed a body. And this is the primary agenda of God for creating man, which is, that He-God may find a body through which He will express Himself on earth because He—God chooses to be a spirit that cannot directly interact with the earth realm without a body. Therefore, man's body is a temple of the Holy ghost where the spirit of God dwells and manifest Himself on earth."

Beloved shook his head in understanding and muttered to himself "1 Corinthians 6:19".

"Now let me introduce you to man," the Celestial Being continued. He brought Beloved before the entity named 'Body'. "This is my body, the body of man. It is that part of man that gives man world-consciousness because it is with this corporal body that man comes into contact with the material world- this earth realm. It is the physical part of man that can be seen, felt and touched by senses. It is inside this body that other components of man like spirit and soul dwell. This body is the mortality in man, the part of man that dies-ceases to live. And anything within the soul and spirit is expressed by the body if so wished by man. The body is the seat of senses."

"So the body is the conduit?" asked Beloved.

"Yes Beloved," confirmed the Celestial Being. "It is most definitely the channel through which the things in man are carried out."

They moved further to the other entities. "Now before I reveal the soul to you, let me introduce you to the divinity in man." said the Celestial Being as he brought Beloved before the entity named 'Spirit'. "This part of man is called the spirit. it is divine and impalpable that is, cannot be seen or touched. It is the breath of life from God that became man's spirit and quickened the lifeless body to life. This life is not the life of God received at regeneration. It is just a life from God to bring the lifeless body to life. As you read it in Job 33:4 that the breath of the almighty gives me life. This spirit in man is the element of God-consciousness because it is that part by which man communes with God, and by which man apprehends and worships God as God is spirit and those that worship him must worship him in spirit. Man's spirit has three parts: the conscience, intuition and communion. Conscience is the discerning organ that distinguishes right from wrong and it is not subject to the influence of the information stored in the mind. It is therefore independent and direct. It will always be guilty to do and in doing wrong and be justified to do and in doing right. It was this conscience that was being referred to when David said in Psalm 51 verse 10, 'Renew a right spirit within me'. It was this same conscience that was referenced to when it was said about the Apostle Paul in Acts 17 verse 16 that 'his spirit was provoked within him as he saw that the city was full of idols.' That is, there was a discernment and judgement in his spirit-conscience that idolatry was wrong."

"Does that mean this conscience part of the spirit is always right?" Beloved asked as he pondered on the functions of the conscience and how it works in men.

"Yes, in as much as it is alive." replied the Celestial Being. "A man with his spirit in him may confidently and without guilt do, cover and justify his wicked and evil deeds as Cain who killed his brother Abel did when he answered God in this manner 'Am I my brother's keeper?' A response that showed that he was not guilty for having done such a wicked act of killing his brother. When a man is like this, his spirit which functions conscientiously is dead. And that is the status that every man inherited from Adam before regeneration."

"What then is the function of intuition?" asked Beloved who was becoming very curious.

And the Celestial Being answered, "Intuition is the sensing organ of human spirit and it is different from physical sense and soulical sense. That means, any knowledge that does not emanate from a man's soul nor his body comes intuitively. For instance the things and person of God and of the Holy ghost are revealed to believers through their intuition. So when a believer has a knowing in his spirit, it is through intuition part of his spirit. It is this intuition that was being referred to when it is said in the scripture—1 Corinthians 2:11 that 'what man knows the things of a man, save the spirit of man which is in him?'

Beloved then asked, "And the third part?"

"The third part of a man's spirit is communion," responded the Celestial Being. "it is by this that man communicates, fellowships and worships God because the organs of soul like emotions which some believers use to worship God is not adequate to worship God since God is spirit so it is with our spirit part of communion that we must worship him. So when the Apostle Paul said in the Opening address of his letter to the Romans that 'For God is my witness, whom I serve with my spirit' and in his letter to the Corinthians said 'I will sing in the spirit', it is by this communion function of his spirit that such activities were/are to be carried out."

"Romans 1:9 and 1 Corinthians 14:15" muttered Beloved to himself.

"Discerning and judging between right and wrong which is done by the conscience of a man's spirit, is in accordance with the knowing in the intuition part of a man's spirit. And the functions of intuition and communion are also intertwined in that the knowledge of God which man gets during communion with God is revealed to man in the intuition. All this reveals that man's spirit is independent of his soul and body. Also, man's spirit is not the same as the Holy Spirit. Man's spirit is a life-spirit from God while the Holy Spirit is Ruach-Elohim-the spirit of God the same that moved upon the face of the waters when darkness was upon the face of the deep. In acknowledgment of this fact, the Apostle of the Gentiles in Romans 8:16 wrote that it is the Spirit himself-Holy Spirit bearing witness with our spirit-man's spirit that we are children of God." the Celestial Being added.

With that, Beloved gave a sigh.

The Celestial Being continued as they moved to the third entity, "The soul is man's element of self-consciousness in that man is made conscious of his existence by the work of his soul. This soul is the seat of man's personality. Everything that makes man human such as intellect, thoughts, emotions, ideal, love, choice, decision are all experiences of the soul. The constituents of man's soul-personality are the three main faculties of Volition—which is the faculty of man's will; Mind—which is man's faculty of reasoning, memory and intellect; and Emotion—which is man's faculty of feeling.

"Volition, mind and emotion" said Beloved after the Celestial Being.

"Yes." Replied the Celestial Being and continued, "Now to your question on why soul was necessary. Man was to be created in the likeness of God for a reason best known to God. Therefore, man must be a person and not a robot because God is not a robot on automation, but a person who has His own intelligence, wisdom, understanding, emotion and essentially His own will that He can exercise as He wants as He says in the scripture, I will have mercy on whom I will have mercy."

"And I will have compassion on whom I will have compassion. Romans 9:15" Beloved responded.

"That's right" remarked the Celestial Being. "In order for man to have the personality of his own capable of exercising his will just like God, Soul which is the seat of his personality—the house of his will was produced. More also, Spirit and body which is flesh cannot directly interact because spirit is divine and flesh is earthly and there is a standing ceaseless war between the two such that the scripture establishes that 'the flesh lusts against the Spirit, and the Spirit against the flesh: and these are contrary the one to the other: so that ye cannot do the things that ye would'."

"That's Galatians 5:17." confirmed Beloved who was scripturally following the Celestial Being's expositions.

The Celestial Being nodded in acknowledgement of Beloved efforts regarding the scriptures and continued, "Because of this enmity between spirit and body, there was a reaction when man's spirit came in contact with the body which necessitated the production of an entity 'Soul' that would serve as an interface between the two. Now by this soul, man can exercise his will on whether to yield to the divine-spirit or the earthly-body which is also flesh. Therefore, man by creation was made up of two different entities, the body-corporeal and the spirit-spiritual. But when God placed the spiritual within corporeal, the soul was produced. The spirit of man touching the lifeless body produced the soul. And with this, you can call man a tripartite being comprised of spirit, soul and body. God dwells in the spirit, self dwells in the soul, while senses dwell in the body."

Beloved interjected, "Glory to God in heaven!"

The Celestial Being held Beloved hand again and they vanished from the effigy and landed outside the fence-like cloud in front of the effigy.

"Aww!" Beloved expressed in surprise.

"With all these, I expect you to know by now that man is not a spirit." stated the Celestial Being.

"But the scripture says God created man in his own image and likeness and that God is spirit. If indeed God is spirit and God created man is his own image and likeness, wouldn't it be tantamount to saying man is not in the image and likeness of God, if one says man is not spirit as God is?" Beloved inquired.

The Celestial Being responded, "When God said let's make man in our image and likeness, he was not talking about making man as the person of God which is spirit, but rather in the form and capacity of God. That's why of all creatures, man is the only creature that has the same form or call it look as God. And because of this, the appearance of God is most times in man's version. Thus when the Lord appeared unto Abraham in Genesis 18, His appearance with the two others was that of man so that scripture says 'And the Lord appeared unto him in the plains of Mamre: and he sat in the tent door in the heat of the day. And he lift up his eyes and looked, and, lo, three men stood by him'. Not because God is a man, but because the form or appearance of God is in His making, as the form or appearance of man; not of beasts, not of plants not of rocks. Man is also in the likeness of God in capacity, in that God has dominion over all things and so He created man in the likeness of His dominion. Scriptures establish that God is a God of dominion. Job 25:2."

"Dominion and fear are with him, Psalms 103:22." added Beloved.

"Bless the Lord, all his works in all places of his dominion. Psalm 145:13." added the Celestial Being.

"Thy kingdom is an everlasting kingdom, and thy dominion endures throughout all generations. Jude 1:25." Beloved further added.

Both Beloved and the Celestial Being echoed, "To the only wise God our Saviour, be glory and majesty, dominion and power, both now and ever." As they echoed that, a great and very bright light shone upon them. Its effulgence was such that kept their faces down as they couldn't look at it for a while until its radiation shifted away from their faces, just then they continued their conversation.

The Celestial Being continued, "in the likeness of this His dominion created He man for He expressly states that it is for the reason of having dominion that man should be created in his image and likeness. That's Genesis 1:26, 'And God said, Let us make man in our image, after our likeness: and let them have dominion over the fish of the sea, and over the fowl of the air, and over the cattle, and over all the earth, and over every creeping thing that creeps upon the earth'."

Upon that enlightenment Beloved said, "Hmm! So that's why David in his song in Psalms 8:4-8 says, 'What is man, that thou art mindful of him? and the son of man, that thou visits him? For thou hast made him a little lower than the angels, and hast crowned him with glory and honour. Thou made him to have dominion over the works of thy hands; thou hast put all things under his feet. All sheep and oxen, yea, and the beasts of the field; The fowl of the air, and the fish of the sea, and whatsoever passes through the paths of the seas'."

"Yes Beloved." The Celestial Being responded. "Therefore, man is not as the person of God for the person of God is spirit as the scriptures say, 'God is spirit' and also that 'Now the Lord is that spirit'. Even man is not as the covering of God for the covering of God is light. As it is written, 'The Lord wraps himself in light as with a garment, Psalms 104:2. So also it is written that 'He dwells in unapproachable light' just as he created men to dwell in a body—1 Timothy 6:16 and 1 John 1:5 also bears record that God is light." The Celestial Being paused.

They moved down the road for a while. Beloved was staring at the look of where they were, it was such that he hadn't seen and such that he couldn't describe. He had many questions to ask about the place but before he would ask one, he would see another thing worthy of inquiry and that was so overwhelming that he couldn't help but concentrate on the spiritual insights that was being given him by the Celestial Being.

"To further establish that man is not a spirit, what the scripture says is not that man is spirit but rather that there is a spirit in man Job 32:8. That is, inside of man, there is a spirit in him. Also Jesus clarified this in Luke 24:39 when he appeared to his disciples after his resurrection and his disciples thought they had seen a spirit, Jesus gave a statement that 'See my hands and my feet, that it is I myself. Touch me, and see. For a spirit does not have flesh and bones as you see that I have.' If a spirit does not have flesh and bones and man has both flesh and bones, it is then settled that man is not spirit." The Celestial Being gave more justification.

"Wow! What then is man?" Asked Beloved who was at the point was more curious.

And the Celestial Being replied, 'First of, man is dust which is flesh in material or call it covering. So we have scripture like Gen 3:19 that says 'for dust thou art, and unto dust shalt thou return.' Even Abraham reckoned with this when he said 'Now that I have been so bold as to speak to the Lord, though I am nothing but dust and ashes'—Gen 18:27."

Beloved nodded his head in understanding and asked, "Oh! So that was why God called man flesh when he said my spirit shall no more strive with men, for he also is flesh right?"

"You're right Beloved." The Celestial Being answered. "However, the person of man is soul, man is soul for his personality is in the soul. Man is predominantly a living soul because Man not only has a body with the breath of life but also became a living soul as well. Thus we find later in the Scriptures that God often referred to men as 'souls'. For instance, God said in Genesis 17:14, 'And the uncircumcised man child whose flesh of his foreskin is not circumcised, that soul shall be cut off from his people'. Because what the man is, depends on how his soul is. His soul represents him and expresses his individuality. That's why scripture says 'the first Adam who was made a living soul—1 Corinthians 15:45."

Then Beloved inquired, "In your house the other time—the house of man, you showed me the three entities that man is composed of which are body, soul and spirit. If I may ask, what is their hierarchy? What is their order of magnitude and value?"

"Maybe we should get to a place" replied the Celestial Being.

"What place?" Beloved asked

"The temple" the Celestial Being responded.

"Why the temple?" Beloved further asked.

"Because you will not understand the answer to that question perfectly unless you see the temple."

Beloved was about to ask further questions when the Celestial Being cut in, "Just come with me".

3 THE TEMPLE

Back in the fellowship, Alice had organized a group of intercessors who prayed fervently for the fellowship and for the President, even though they were unaware of what had been going on with the president. They met frequently praying for answer to all the recent confusions in the fellowship, and also prayed as they were led by the Holy Spirit.

In their journey, Beloved and the Celestial Being arrived before an ancient temple, very beautiful and full of splendor and treasures.

"This is the heavenly prototype of the temple of God built by Solomon for God according to the pattern which King David his father received of the Lord." said the Celestial Being.

Wow! It's magnificent!" remarked Beloved as he kept staring and admiring the grandeur of the temple.

The Celestial Being had to continue with his assignment of illuminating Beloved and so he interrupted Beloved's moments of deep admiration, "The temple is divided into three parts. The first where we are now, is the Outer Court which all can see and where all can stay and offer external worships." They move inside the temple into the next place. "This is the second part. It is called the Holy Place- which is immediately behind the veil covering the third part. Only the Levites—priests can enter this Holy Place and here, they offer more deeper worship than in the outer court. For instance, they present oil, incense and bread to God."

"If only priests can enter here, how am I able to enter?" Beloved questioned.

"Because you're a priest. What do 1 Peter 2 verse 5 and 9 call you?" the Celestial Being asked.

"Verse 5 says "I also, as lively stones, am built up a spiritual house, an holy priesthood, to offer up spiritual sacrifices, acceptable to God by Jesus Christ. Verse 9 says I am a chosen generation, a royal priesthood, an holy nation, a peculiar people; that I should shew forth the praises of him who hath called you out of darkness into his marvelous light." Beloved replied.

"And Revelation 1 verse 6?" asked the Celestial Being.

"He has made us kings and priests unto God and his Father." replied Beloved.

They move into the third part of the temple. "This is the third part and the most deepest part of the temple. It is called the Holy of Holies where God dwells. As you can see, a brilliant light radiates here, it is the presence of God. However, no man can enter. Though the high priest did enter in once annually."

"How then are we able to enter?" asked Beloved.

The Celestial Being answered, " Remember the veil of this temple rent when Jesus died."

"Oh yes! I can remember." Beloved responded. "So, by this all through Jesus can enter into the presence of God."

"You're right Beloved. You now have boldness to enter into the holiest by the blood of Jesus" the Celestial Being remarked.

"Hebrews 10:19." Beloved confirmed.

The Celestial Being continued, "So directions, instructions, leadings and guidance all come from God in the Holy of Holies to the priests in the Holy Place and from the Holy Place to the people in the Outer Court. That is, temple service moves according to the revelation in the Holy of Holies and all activities in the Holy Place and in the Outer Court are regulated by the presence of God in the Holy of Holies."

"So, it is the Holy of Holies that governs the whole temple?" inquired Beloved who was getting better understanding of the matter.

"Yes Beloved!" the Celestial Being confirmed. "Remember that the Apostle Paul reveals that man is God's temple and that God's Spirit dwells in him?"

"Yes! Yes! 1Corinthian 3:16" Beloved answered.

And the Celestial Being continued, "Man is also God's temple and he has three parts too. The body is like the Outer Court, that is visible to all. Inside the body is man's soul which is as the Holy Place because it is the seat of man's personality that no one can see or know except man himself and the great high priest God, who knows the heart of men. Innermost, behind the veil, is the Holy of Holies into which no human light has ever penetrated and no naked eye has ever pierced. It is "the secret place of the Most High," the dwelling place of God. It cannot be reached by man unless God is willing to rend the veil. It is man's spirit with which man unites and communes with God."

Beloved nodded his head and said, "if man is the temple of God and man's spirit is the Holy of Holies, that means the same way the Holy of Holies governs the whole temple is the same way the spirit of a man should govern the whole man."

"That is it Beloved." reaffirmed the Celestial Being. "As the Holy of Holies is the highest court of the temple is the same way the spirit of a man is the highest part of him. After it comes the soul which is as the Holy Place and after soul comes body which is as the Outer Court. With this, you understand the hierarchy of the components of man in the eyes of God. Scripture confirms the order in 2 Thessalonians 5:23 when it says, 'Now may the God of peace himself sanctify you completely, and may your whole spirit and soul and body be kept blameless at the coming of our Lord Jesus Christ'."

Immediately the Celestial Being ended that last statement, the temple vanished away from their sight. Whilst they were moving away from that location, the Celestial Being began to reveal some other things to Beloved, "Now let's consider the state of man as created by God," said the Celestial Being. "As God created man, the spirit is the highest component followed by the soul and then the body. In that state, the power of man's soul was completely under the dominion of his spirit. And man was ignorant of the striving of the flesh and spirit not because the striving was not there but because man was in a perfect state and had not tasted of the works of the flesh by which such striving will be brought into his knowledge, experience and reality. Also at that state, man was not ignorant of his spirituality because man did commune with God and had the knowledge of the voice of God and the presence of God, as it was later revealed in the book of Genesis 3:8, how man and his wife hid themselves from the presence of God. At that time, whenever God walked into the garden and stand over there, man's spirit would perceive it, the soul would have no choice but to respond to it since the soul was under the dominion of the spirit, and the body also would yield in subjection to that fellowship. For the spirit was like a mistress, the soul like a steward, and the body like a servant. The mistress committed matters to the steward who in turn commanded the servant to carry them out."

"Okay! The master exercises the control." noted Beloved.

The Celestial Being continued, "God kept coming to man so as to make man love him by keeping his words, and walking with him to a point where man will access that light in God that will illuminate him and open his eyes to the tree of life that he may eat and live forever. That's why that scripture says 'in him was life and the life was the light of men'. So, God was waiting for man to manifest his will to choose either life or death because he has told man that the tree of the knowledge of good and evil is death. Even creature that was made subject to vanity was awaiting the manifestation of the sons of God in Adam and Eve only if they would choose the tree of life. So, I was leaving in obedience to the word of God in the garden, abstaining from the tree of the knowledge of good and evil until that day... that day... that day.. when that apocalyptic choice was made." The Celestial Being sighed and bowed down his head.

"Please tell me about it. What really happened that day?" queried Beloved.

"The time to depart from you is at hand." answered the Celestial Being.

"No! No! No! It cannot end here. There's still some more I need to know. Lord have mercy!" Beloved pleaded.

The Celestial Being nodded his head in pity and walked ahead, leaving Beloved who was crying for mercy behind.

4 THE GARDEN OF EDEN & THE FALL OF MAN

"Oh Lord have mercy, it can't end here there's more. Lord have mercy." Beloved continued pleading on his knees.

Not quite long, the Celestial Being appeared beside him again, "Your cry has been heard. Now come with me let's see how man fell." said the Celestial Being.

Beloved was happy to hear that and immediately, he rose to continue the journey with the Celestial Being, "where are we going now?" he asked.

"To the garden of Eden." answered the Celestial Being. Immediately he said that, they were caught away and found themselves in a very beautiful and serene garden with several fruits, trees and animals.

Beloved couldn't help but wondered at the splendor of the garden, "oh my God!"

As though he had just a little time to spend with Beloved, the Celestial Being started immediately, "As you now know, Satan was the first occupant of this garden but was sent out when iniquity was found in him. So when he saw that another entity is now inhabiting the garden, he knew that there was a problem for him, knowing that this entity called man is to dominate, subdue and rule the earth realm as God; and Satan is on earth for he was cast to the earth after his rebellion."

"Oh! Revelation 12:9 'And the great dragon was cast out, that old serpent, called the Devil, and Satan, which deceives the whole world: he was cast out into the earth, and his angels were cast out with him'." Beloved confirmed.

The Celestial Being continued, "That is why the garden of Eden is not a geographical location on earth. You cannot find it anywhere on earth because it is not a location on earth rather it is a realm of God. It is called the garden of God that God planted on earth. So, Genesis 2:8 says 'And the Lord God planted a garden eastward in Eden'. So when devil was there, the realm was in heaven and when God created man and decided that earth will be man's sphere of influence, He had to download that realm called garden of God to the earth and planted it at a region called Eden, so that man can keep it which means man can retain & preserve it by making the other parts of earth look like it. Thus, God gave man the task of keeping and dressing the garden. Since Satan is on earth and man's divine mandate is to subdue and dominate the earth and everything therein including Satan, Satan had to find a way to prevent that from happening. And he came up with a plan to make man do that same thing he did that made God sent him out of the garden of God which is to desire to be as God. That's why what he said to lure eve in Genesis 3:5 was 'ye shall be as God knowing good and evil'."

Beloved who was actively and attentively following the exposition, nodded his head in such a manner that showed he was grasping the revelation.

Then the Celestial Being went on, "And Satan knew he had to act fast before man will journey in koinonia with God to a stage where his eyes will be opened by illumination from God to the tree of life and thereby eat it and live with the life of God-incorruption and immortal forever. Let's watch how Satan deceived Eve."

The three entities namely; spirit, soul and body came to their view in the garden. "These are the spirit, soul and body of Eve shortly before the fall in this garden." said the Celestial Being. Beloved was surprised to see an open display of the fall of man.

The Celestial Being continued, "The only person that Adam and Eve knew was God and then the living creatures in the garden, so if Satan had come in his own form, Eve and Adam might have run away from such a stranger or even raise an alarm and summon God to come to their aid. So Satan in his wiles decided to come through the most subtle beast of the field that they were familiar with in the garden which is the serpent. I can say that the reason why Satan came to Eve and not Adam was because of seniority. Adam preceded the serpent not on earth but in the garden and if the serpent had come to Adam, I would most likely shut the serpent up saying you met me here, it was me and God before God made you when he saw that I needed help, who are you to give counsel about God and the garden to me? But the serpent had been in the garden before Eve came, so Satan came to Eve with the view that Eve would possibly listen to the serpent because it was more experienced than her as far as life in the garden was concerned. So on that day, Eve was somewhere in the garden and Satan came in as a serpent."

Beloved and the Celestial Being were watching, while a serpent from the garden came directly to the soul-entity of Eve, that is, the soul of Eve.

"Why did the serpent come unto the soul of Eve and not the body or spirit?" Beloved questioned.

And the Celestial Being replied, "You know Satan is wise in his own conceit. He wanted to make sure that man and not he was responsible for that act of disobedience, so he came to the seat of her person where her will is, even as he knew that God has given man the freewill of choosing either life or death and he knew whatsoever man chose, God would respect the choice. Naturally, a serpent being an animal could not talk, but being possessed by Satan, he began to incite Eve's soul against the counsel of God."

The serpent then began to question Eve's soul, "Has God said, Ye shall not eat of every tree of the garden?"

"We may eat of the fruit of the trees of the garden. But of the fruit of the tree which is in the midst of the garden, God hath said, we shall not eat of it, neither shall we touch it, lest we die." replied Eve in her soul.

The Celestial Being quickly drew Beloved's attention, "You see Beloved, this is how Satan works in the life of man. He cannot work in isolation, he works on the information in a man's mind. That's why when he came to Jesus, the first thing he said was 'if thou be the son of God'. Remember the information that Jesus is the son of God was given when Jesus was coming out of the water after his baptism?"

"Yes, Yes! Matthew 3:17, 'And lo a voice from heaven, saying, This is my beloved Son, in whom I am well pleased'." Beloved responded.

"That is it." Confirmed the Celestial Being. "And it was immediately thereafter that He was taken to the wilderness by the spirit to fast and pray forty days and forty night. And Satan who is the devil, having got that information at Jesus' baptism, came to remind Him of that information and used it to set a trap that Jesus escaped. The lesson of those two encounters is that it is not enough to have a light from every word or information that you catch in God, that light must shine so much bright that darkness will not be able to comprehend it. Jesus's light shines so bright that the devil in all his wiles and deception could not comprehend Him, even when he came to Him in Peter. Jesus later made a statement that the prince of this world comes and has no power over me."

"Oh!" remarked Beloved.

"Beloved, let's see further." said the Celestial Being as they kept watching what transpired between the Satan-possessed serpent and Eve.

The Satan-possessed serpent then said to Eve "You shall not surely die, For God knows that when you eat from it your eyes will be opened, and you will be like God, knowing good and evil."

After that word from the serpent, the serpent left and the body-entity that is, the body of Eve moved closer to the tree of the knowledge of good and evil in the garden, staring at the fruit. Later the soul-entity, that is, the soul of Eve also drew to the fruit and after a long consideration and determination in the soul to eat of the tree, the body plucked the fruit of the tree and ate it.

"Can you see the mistake that Eve made, she thought in her heart that Satan might be right. Therefore her soul considered what Satan said, that caused her body to move closer to the tree to examine the fruit of the tree with her eyes. Her eyes of understanding was not enlightened enough for her to know that the devil does not stand in the truth because there is no truth in him. When he lies, he speaks out of his own character: for he is a liar, and the father of lies." Commented the Celestial Being.

"Oh! John 8:44. So had she caught this light, she would have told the devil 'get the off me' immediately as Jesus did." said Beloved.

"Yes Beloved." responded the Celestial Being. "Satan has three major instruments he uses to operate: lies, deception and ignorance. He deployed all the three on Eve. He lied to Eve that if she eats the tree of the knowledge of good and evil, she shall not surely die when eventually she died to God after eating it. He deceived her as if knowing good and evil is the best state of being as God when indeed it is the eternal life of God which is in the tree of life; and he took advantage of Eve's ignorance of his true identity. You can see that in all her consideration, her spirit—her organ of God-consciousness was not carried along. Eve had a choice of exercising her will to yield to the spirit which would have guided her through intuition to discern the deceit of the devil and through conscience to make the right choice of obeying God by abstaining from the forbidden fruit; or to yield to the body-flesh which would guide her through the lusts thereof to do that which is contrary to God. Unfortunately, Eve yielded to the flesh in that she considered that which Satan sowed into her soul in the flesh. Therefore she beheld the fruit by her senses which are the organs of her body and was guided by the lusts thereof first of, the lust of the flesh, by which she saw that the tree was good for food and the lust of the eyes by which she saw that it was pleasant to the eyes. And then her soul was enticed. It was not merely the lust of the flesh and the lust of the eyes, but also curiosity's urge for soulical wisdom which is an act of rebellion to God called pride of life—by which she saw that it was a tree to be desired to make one wise. Thus, Satan provoked her soulical thought and in response, Eve changed the order of spirit, soul and body and started from the body and to the soul. Her soul was now agitated beyond control. So in sum, when the woman saw that the tree was good for food, and that it was a delight to the eyes, and that the tree was to be desired to make one wise, she took of its fruit and ate."

"Ah! That's pathetic!" Beloved reacted. "What of Adam?"

"I, Adam obviously was not deceived" replied the Celestial Being. "As the Apostle Paul puts it in 1 Timothy 2:14—Adam was not the one deceived; it was the woman who was deceived and deluded and fell into transgression. Also, according to the record of Genesis it is written that 'the woman said, the serpent beguiled me and I ate' but that 'the man said, the woman gave (not beguiled) me fruit of the tree and I ate' Gen. 3:12-13."

"Aha!" Beloved reacted.

The Celestial Being said further, "So, his mind was clear and he knew the fruit was from the forbidden tree. He ate because of his affection for the woman. Adam understood that what the serpent said was nothing more than the enemy's deception. From the words of the Apostle, you will understand that Adam sinned deliberately. He loved Eve more than himself. He made her his idol, and for her sake he was willing to rebel against the commandment of his Creator. That means, his mind was overruled by his emotion; his reasoning, overcome by his affection and so guided solely by his soul rather than the spirit, he ate the fruit and fell. Adam didn't know that what man become with his wife after cleaving to her is one flesh and not one soul. This means it is not by force or compulsion that the state of their souls be the same such that if one chooses to follow the gods of this world, it is not a must that the other must follow them too. 1 Peter 3:1 says that even if husbands do not obey the word of God, wives must obey the word of God by being submissive to their husbands. And not to join their husband in having a heart of disobedience, even though they are still one flesh."

At this point, Beloved sighed, "what an insight!" he said and questioned further, "So, what happened to the spirit, soul and body after this fall?"

The Celestial Being responded, "According to the word of God that in the day that man eat of the tree of the knowledge of good and evil man shall die, having eaten the fruit of the tree, Adam's spirit died because of his disobedience to God. He still had his spirit, yet it was dead to God for it had lost its spiritual instinct. Sin has destroyed the spirit's keen intuitive knowledge of God and rendered man spiritually dead. He may be religious, moral, learned, capable, strong and wise, but he is dead to God. He may even talk about God, reason about God and preach God, but he is still dead to Him. Man is not able to hear or to sense the voice of God's Spirit. As his spirit died, man was plunged into darkness because the spirit of a man that died is the candle of the Lord, the light that lights the man—Proverbs 20:27."

"Oh my God!" Beloved exclaimed.

The Celestial Being continued, "Man's body, which could have been transformed and glorified, was instead returned to dust. Because his inward man had fallen into chaos, his outward body must die and be destroyed. From that day, Adam's spirit as well as the spirit of all his descendants, fell under the oppression of the soul. Thus, after the fall, the spirit of man lost his dominion over the soul and consequently the whole man and soul gained dominion over the spirit and consequently over the whole man. However, the soul is not merely independent of the spirit; it is additionally under the body's control in yielding to the demand of its passions and lusts. Fallen men are governed completely by the flesh, walking in response to the desires of their soulish life and physical passions. Such ones are unable to commune with God. Sometimes they display their intellect, at others times their passion, but more often both their intellect and passion. Unimpeded, the flesh is in firm control over the total man. This state of a man is abnormal for man has now descended from 'spirit-control' to 'soul-control,' and from 'soul-control' to 'body-control.' In sum, Sin has slain the spirit: spiritual death hence becomes the portion of all, for all are dead in sins and trespasses. Sin has rendered the soul independent: the soulish life is therefore but a selfish and self-willed one. Sin has finally empowered the body: sinful nature accordingly reigns through the body. And finally, the hope that man will come in contact with the life of God was lost as man was sent out of the garden of God-Eden. And the garden was taken away from earth and God set cherubim and flaming sword round about it so that man will not by the help of some illegal spirit be transported into the garden of God-Eden and eat of the tree of life and live forever. That's why there are several historic places of Biblical reference on earth but for garden of Eden. Because the garden as I said earlier is not a geographical location on earth, it is a realm that was downloaded to earth and taken up after the fall of men. The most that can be found about the garden is where it was situated while on earth which is eastward in Eden."

Beloved who was so touched commented, "My God! That's dishearte..."

And before he could finish saying 'disheartening', they were transported back to the earth realm in Beloved's room.

5 ENCOUNTER WITH THE LAST ADAM

"What? We are back to earth realm?" asked Beloved who was quite surprised to find them back to his room. He was in the same position and condition as he was before they were caught up. Only that this time, he looked more weak and tired.

"Yes Beloved." The Celestial Being responded, "what is most disheartening is that my time is up, I have to depart from you."

"Depart? But I haven't found the answer to my inquiry" Beloved expressed in dissatisfaction.

"Beloved! I have not come to give you the answer," the Celestial Being replied. "I have only come to place you in a right position to getting the answer. I have given you an understanding of man that why man acts the way he acts is not the function of his temperament as it were, rather it is the function of his components which I have enlightened you on. Howbeit, when the answer comes, you will understand better. You need to tarry here in prayer and meditation until the answer comes, for you know not the hour of your visitation. But I see weakness and weariness all over you. Always remember that you're compassed about with so great a cloud of witnesses. Shalom!!!"

As soon as Celestial Being said this, he was taken away from the room—Alas! It was an open vision.

Beloved was lying there on the floor. He was so weak and tired, it has been 47 days of fasting as the encounter with the Celestial Being lasted for seven days.

"Have mercy Lord! Have mercy Lord! My spirit is willing but this flesh is weak. I really want to leave and go for refreshments now but I cannot leave here without getting the answer. I cannot afford to have my labour be in vain. Please help me Lord!" He cried.

He did not have strength to talk very well so he groaned while he muttered "Oh Lord give life to my spirit, give life to my mind and quicken my mortal body."

And while he was saying that repeatedly, he dozed off.

The intercessory group in the fellowship kept praying earnestly for the president and for the fellowship. Normal fellowship services continued and the duties of Beloved as the President and Pastor of the fellowship were being carried out by the brothers' coordinator—Thomas. Expectedly, the fellowship was experiencing drastic reduction in membership due to the escalation of the scandal. Most especially, Debbie's fresh involvement in another scandal after excommunicating herself from the fellowship. The thought that the fellowship prayer coordinator, could continue in such ungodly acts was what most members could not deal with and as such, had to leave the fellowship.

Two days later, Beloved who had been lying on the floor sleeping intermittently, woke up from his slumber to continue praying seriously. "Lord send the answer! You say I should call upon you and you will answer me and show me great and mighty things which I know not oh Lord I cry to you for answer".

Later, he stood from the floor and sat at the table to study. He had hardly studied for four hours when he put his head on the table and dozed off again.

One hour later, the was a very heavy footsteps approaching Beloved door. On getting to the door, the door opened of its own accord and a Being full of lights shining beyond what eyes could behold, with a countenance as of fire and with a golden crown on the head, entered his room whilst he was fast asleep. The Being came in bearing a tray that had a slice of bread and a cup of red liquid in it. The Being placed the tray on the table and sat on the chair at the table which was opposite the one Beloved was sitting on and then began to speak, "In the beginning was the Word, and the Word was with God, and the Word was God. He was in the beginning with God. All things were made by him; and without him was not anything made that was made. In him was life; and the life was the light of men. And the light shines in darkness; and the darkness comprehended it not. There was a man sent from God, whose name was John. The same came for a witness, to bear witness of the Light, that all men through him might believe. He was not that Light, but was sent to bear witness of that Light. That was the true Light, which lights every man that comes into the world. He was in the world, and the world was made by him, and the world knew him not. He came unto his own, and his own received him not. But as many as received him, to them he gave power to become the sons of God, even to them that believe on his name. Which were born, not of blood, nor of the will of the flesh, nor of the will of man, but of God. And the Word was made flesh, and dwelt among us, and we beheld his glory, the glory as of the only begotten of the Father, full of grace and truth."

Just there, Beloved who could hear the voice of the Being loud in his sleep raised up his head and look at the direction of that Being sitting in front of him but could not behold it. So, he put his face back on the table and even cover it with his hand as the face shone. "Fear not son" the Being stated.

"who are you?" Beloved asked.

The Being didn't answer but rather said to him, "lift up your head"

"I can't look at the countenance of your face, because it is like lightning." replied Beloved.

"Blessed are the pure in heart, for they shall see God. Behold and believe, and you shall see me" the Being said.

Beloved slowly raised up his head and beheld the face of the Being.

The Being took the bread and broke it and offered it to Beloved, "Eat."

"No, I won't eat." said Beloved.

"Eat son" the Being insisted.

And Beloved replied, "I have bound myself that I will not drink nor eat until I get the answer to the perplexity of my heart"

"You need to eat Beloved, for the Journey is far, it is an unleavened bread." said the Being.

And Beloved, considering his weakness and on getting to know that the journey is far, took the bread from the Being and ate.

"They that wait upon the Lord shall renew their strength; they shall mount up with wings as eagles; they shall run, and not be weary; and they shall walk, and not faint." stated the Being and he took the cup containing some red liquid, muttered some words of thanks and offered it to Beloved. "Take drink all of it." The Being offered.

Beloved took the cup and drank half of it and put the rest down on the table.

"I said drink all" the Being insisted.

"You should drink too and have the other bread. I should not forgetful to entertain strangers but since you're the one that brought something, it is good that we share it." Beloved responded.

And the Being replied, "No, you take it all, you need to be strengthened to get the answer remember"

"That's true. Thank you." said Beloved as he picked the other half of the bread, ate it and took the cup to drink the remaining content.

"I cannot drink anymore of this fruit of the vine, until that day when I drink it new with you in my father's kingdom." said the Being.

Having heard that, Beloved suddenly dropped the cup from his mouth, "Who are you again?" he asked.

The Being smiled and answered, "I am the Last Adam"

"a quickening spirit?" asked Beloved, who had become very familiar and frequent with that scripture.

"Yes Beloved. In me shall all be made alive." the Being replied.

Beloved began to meditate on that statement, "In you shall all be made alive...Hmm! For as in Adam all died, even so in Christ shall all be made alive... In Christ shall all be made alive, in Christ... In Christ. Wait... You're Christ?" he asked.

"Yes, I am Christ" the Being replied.

"You're Jesus?" Beloved further asked.

And the Being replied, "Yes Beloved. I am Jesus Christ, the son of the living God.

Beloved jumped up in excitement and wonder, alas! It has been Jesus all the while. Beloved couldn't keep how surprised he was to himself, "oh! My

Saviour Lord. My king, Lord of Lords, king of kings, Prince of peace, in my room?

Jesus smiled and responded in the affirmative.

"Oh my God! I wish I could touch you right now, but I remember you restrained Mary Magdalene from touching you." stated Beloved.

Jesus replied, "You can hold on to me now, for I have ascended unto my father your father, my God your God."

Then Jesus stood up and Beloved came to him and bowed to kiss his feet and then embraced him with so much excitement.

And Jesus said, "The cry of your brethren could not make me tarry to come."

"My brethren In the fellowship?" asked Beloved.

"Yes." Jesus affirmed. "The first man Adam was here?"

"Yes Lord! But he could not give me the answer." Beloved replied.

Jesus then asked him, "Do you know why he couldn't give you the answer?

Beloved immediately replied, "No Lord! You know all things."

"It is because it was not given him to give the answer. For he is not worthy to open the book and to loose the seals thereof. But rejoice because I the lamb that was slain, the lion of the tribe of Judah, the root of David, the same that holds your hand, I've prevailed to open the book and to loose the seals thereof. I have come to give you the answer." Jesus stated.

And Beloved reacted in appreciation, "Thank you Lord".

"However, the first man Adam has rightfully place you on the right foundation to understanding the answer." Jesus added.

Beloved nodded his head and smiled as Jesus held his hand and continued "Son, this is the answer, let's start from Calvary.

6 CALVARY

As Jesus held Beloved's hand, they both appeared at Golgotha by bilocation. In that experience, Golgotha was as it was when Jesus was hanging on the cross. Beloved could see clearly the Saviour on the cross.

And Jesus began to enlighten his eyes of understanding, "Father couldn't afford to lose man forever, so the loving and merciful God set out to reconcile man back unto Himself."

"Why? Why couldn't God lose man? Why couldn't He in his almighty power and wisdom just destroy men and create maybe another hominoid species that will be loyal and obedient to him?" Beloved queried.

Jesus smiled and answers, "Because of His great and infinite love for man. He so loved man of all His creation that He was not mindful to release His only begotten son to the grave for a while just to save man. So the scriptures bear records and say, 'For God so loved the world, that he gave his only begotten Son, that whosoever believeth in him should not perish, but have everlasting life' (John 3:16). 'But God commends his love toward us, in that, while we were yet sinners, Christ died for us' (Romans 5:8). 'In this was manifested the love of God toward us, because that God sent his only begotten Son into the world, that we might live through him; Herein is love, not that we loved God, but that he loved us, and sent his Son to be the propitiation for our sins' (1 John 4:9-10)."

"Thanks be to God for His love for us. Alleluia!" responded Beloved. "But Lord, why must the only begotten of the Father die to save man?"

Jesus then replied, "man had not paid for his sin of disobedience in the garden. The death of man's spirit and the darkness he was plunged into by eating the tree of the knowledge of good and evil was just a consequence of his choice not the punishment. Even the curse that God placed on man was not the punishment, but the revelation of the wrath of God on man's flesh. There was a standing spiritual law that man violated and man was liable to the punishment under it. That is the law that says, 'the soul that sins shall die', that you will find in the book of Ezekiel 18:4,20. The death here is not the death of man's body, because man's body by virtue of the curse placed on him by God after the fall will surely return back to dust whether regenerated or not regenerated. That means the death here is the perishing of the soul in eternal damnation. The psalmist knew this when he said, 'For thou hast delivered my soul from death' (Psalm 56:13), and that 'Behold, the eye of the Lord is upon them that fear him, upon them that hope in his mercy; To deliver their soul from death' (Psalms 33:18-19). And prophet Esaias while giving the messianic prophesy of Jesus said, 'Incline your ear, and come unto me: hear, and your soul shall live; and I will make an everlasting covenant with you, even the sure mercies of David' (Isaiah 55:3). Likewise, talking about Jesus' work of salvation, Peter—an Apostle enjoined believers in this wise, 'Receiving the end of your faith, even the salvation of your souls.' (1 Peter 1:9). It is thus established, that salvation that was wrought through the death and resurrection of Jesus Christ was to save the souls of men if they can believe, as believing is to the saving of their soul from hell (Hebrews 10:39)."

"Aha!" Beloved exclaimed silently.

"Every man's soul was under the curse of that law in Ezekiel 18:4&20, and the punishment of death must be meted to every man's soul in hell. But God in his love did not and does not want that, so God in His wisdom and sovereignty devised a substitutionary means to make someone else die, that is, make another person suffer that death punishment in place of every man. Therefore He sent me—Jesus, His only begotten son to make that substitutionary sacrifice. And because I and my father are one, His love for man is my love for man, I came down to the earth to die for all, that I might save all from their sins." Jesus added.

"Lord! Why must it be you?" Beloved asked. "God could have just used some animals as in the old testament or chosen one of the prophets to pay the substitutionary sacrifice for us, if it must necessarily be a man."

Jesus answered, "The curse of that law is to man and not animals. So animals couldn't have being a substitute that will redeem man from the curse of that law. 'For it is not possible that the blood of bulls and of goats should take away sins' (Hebrews 10:4), it must therefore be a man. A man must be made a curse for every man in order to redeem them from the curse of that law, and that's the reason it was to be a death on the cross because cursed is every one that hangs on a tree. Therefore, I—Christ being hanged on the cross, was made a curse for you all."

"Oh! Galatians 3:13 'Christ hath redeemed us from the curse of the law, being made a curse for us: for it is written, Cursed is every one that hangs on a tree'." Muttered Beloved to himself as he beheld the cross and the savior on it. "And why not another man maybe one of the prophets?"

"The whole essence of salvation, is to give eternal life which man missed in the tree of life back to men," responded Jesus. "It is only eternal life that can deliver man's soul from hell. And it was not a life that man could give because no man had it, for every man missed it when Adam chose the tree of the knowledge of good and evil instead of the tree of life. Therefore this life is only from God. And God has given it to me His son Jesus Christ to give unto men who believe in me. Many scriptures testify of me saying, 'And this is the record, that God hath given to us eternal life, and this life is in his Son. He that hath the Son hath life; and he that hath not the Son of God hath not life. These things have I written unto you that believe on the name of the Son of God; that ye may know that ye have eternal life, and that ye may believe on the name of the Son of God' (1 John 5:11-13). In the same vein, John bears records of me that I said 'As father hast given me power over all flesh, that I should give eternal life to as many as He hast given me; And I give unto them eternal life; and they shall never perish, neither shall any man pluck them out of my hand' (John 17:2; 10:28). So he must be a man so that he can die the death of the cross, for God cannot die. And he must be God so that he can impart eternal life to men for men cannot impart eternal life. For these reasons, I who was one with God was made flesh, that is, I became man that as Moses lifted up the serpent in the wilderness, even so was I the Son of man lifted up: That whosoever believes in me should not perish, but have eternal life."

There was a deep silence for a couple of minutes. And Jesus continued, "Since you know the state of man after the fall, let's consider what Calvary did to a fallen man. First of all, the work of Calvary has effect only on those who believe in Jesus Christ. Every man who does not believe in Jesus Christ will still remain in his fallen state and have his soul perish in hell. But on the fallen man who believed, Calvary worked regeneration called new birth, by which man passed out of death into life. By this regeneration, God's life was imparted into the spirit of man. Although, by the substitutionary death of Jesus Christ on the cross, man's sins that are passed have been forgiven through the forbearance of God (Roman 3:25), yet his soul is still sinful because it is still the organ of self-consciousness and fulfilling it desires will lead man to destruction. Therefore, regeneration revives man's spirit which is his organ of God-consciousness with God's life through the Holy Spirit, that man may be alive unto God by being entirely controlled by his Holy Spirit- indwelt spirit unto eternal life, and not by the sinful soul again unto destruction. That means, regeneration does not do anything to man's soul neither does it eradicate fleshy lusts from man's body. Rather, it imparts the life of God in the Holy ghost into man's spirit. So now the Holy ghost dwells in man's spirit and guides and direct him according to the will of God. Thus, regeneration was entirely of the spirit of man and not of his soul or body. Man's spirit which died in Adam is now made alive in Christ Jesus as the scripture says, 'For as in Adam all die, even so in Christ shall all be made alive' (1 Corinthians 15:22). I, Jesus Christ, the last Adam is that spirit that quickens the spirit of man back to life. That's why the scriptures say, 'The first man Adam was made a living soul; the last Adam was made a quickening spirit' and 'Now I, the Lord is that Spirit: and where the Spirit of the Lord is, there is liberty'— liberty from self, liberty from flesh."

"Aha!" interjected Beloved, whose eyes has just been opened to the depth of Calvary.

"Beloved! Let this be clear to you now before we leave Calvary," said Jesus, "Regeneration that God the Father used me His son through this Calvary to work in believers, does not remove their soul and body from their components, neither does it make a believer a robot by removing his organ of will, mind and emotion which is his soul. Rather, through the impartation of the life of God, regeneration brings a believer's spirit back to life and separates the soul from the spirit, leaving man with the willpower of choosing whether to be guided by the soul or body—flesh unto death or by the spirit through obeying the leading of the Holy spirit in his spirit unto righteousness, that he—the believer might have his fruit unto Holiness and the end reward—eternal life (Romans 6)."

"Oh! So, the fact that a person is a believer who has experienced new birth does not make him/her unable to commit sins?" asked Beloved.

Jesus smiled and replied, "No it doesn't. It only imparts to him a life that cannot commit sins, if only he will yield with his soul and body to that life imparted. A perpetual act of yielding with his soul and body will bring his soul in oneness with the thought of God and will render the body powerless to fulfill its lusts and affections because man with his soul and body would have become servant to righteousness through obedience to the spirit of God in him. That's why Romans 6:16 says, 'to whom ye yield yourselves servants to obey, his servants ye are to whom ye obey; whether of sin unto death, or of obedience unto righteousness'." Jesus held Beloved hand as He took him away from Calvary."

7 A NATURAL MAN

"Now we are arriving at the answer," said Jesus as he took Beloved to a place like a mountain, more like a pinnacle in the heavenly, where Beloved could see everything happening on earth. "There are three kinds of men: a natural man, a carnal man and a spiritual man." stated Jesus.

"Lord! Who is a natural man?" asked Beloved.

"Every non-regenerated Adam is a natural man," answered Jesus. "A natural man is a man who will not come to Calvary and unto whom the life of God has not been imparted and as such, he is a man who will perish, because it is all foolishness unto him. As the scripture says, 'For the preaching of the cross is to them that perish foolishness' (1 Corinthians1:18). So, every man born of a woman is a natural man. Whether born of a child, prophet or a servant of God, he is by virtue of birth a natural man. Such a man must go through the new birth, that is, must be born of God—a birth that will impart the life of God into him. So that now, he will be able to receive the things of God and to know them for the Spirit of God now dwells in him. For no man knows the things of a man, but the spirit of man which is in him; even so the things of God knows no man, but the Spirit of God (1 Corinthians 2:11). For this reason, the natural man receives not the things of the Spirit of God: for they are foolishness unto him: neither can he know them, because they are spiritually discerned (1 Corinthians 2:14)."

"That means a natural man is a man in his fallen state?" Beloved inquired.

"Yes Beloved," Jesus confirmed. "All men who don't believe in Jesus Christ according to the order of Romans 10:8-10 are only born of the will of man and not born of God. And the wrath of God is upon them until they become born again. To as many as did receive and welcome me, I gave the authority-power, privilege, right to become the children of God, that is, to those who believe in my name—they owe their birth neither to bloods nor to the will of the flesh-that of physical impulse nor to the will of man-that of a natural father, but to God (John 1:12-13 amp)."

"So, all human beings born whether by a regenerated or non-regenerated person are natural men?" Beloved asked to be sure he was getting it.

"Yes Beloved," Jesus reaffirmed. "And it is so because such human beings came as the descendants of the first man Adam who is natural as the scripture puts it, the first was natural and that which came after is spiritual (1 Corinthians 15:46). So all men to be saved from the consequences of their natural life, must come unto Him that came after,—the spiritual that is, Jesus Christ, for in Him is that Spiritual life called eternal life."

"Aha!" exclaimed Beloved.

Jesus continued, "A Natural man finds the things of God to be unreasonable and so he blasphemes, mocks and even makes jest of the things of God in as much as his spirit is dead and suppressed by the soul. His entire life is in darkness, and he is completely governed by his soul and body. As second Peter 2:12 rightly describes them, 'these, as natural brute beasts, made to be taken and destroyed, speak evil of the things that they understand not; and shall utterly perish in their own corruption.' A natural man is not just a mere sinner, he's also a rebel again the things of God in that he refused the life of God and rebellion says the scripture, is as the sin of witchcraft, and the judgement of God is that a witch shall not live (Exodus 22:18). As the life of God is not in natural men, they will always walk in darkness and show forth the work of ungodliness no matter how moral they may be. And as they would not like to retain God in their knowledge, God would give them over to a reprobate mind, to do things which are not convenient. As such, they will be filled with all unrighteousness, fornication, wickedness, covetousness, maliciousness, full of envy, murder, debate, deceit, malignity. They will be whisperers, backbiters, haters of God, despiteful, proud, boasters, inventors of evil things, disobedient to parents, without understanding, covenant breakers, without natural affection, implacable, and unmerciful."

"Can a natural man be in the house of God?" asked Beloved.

"Take a look," said Jesus, as a portion of the earth realm was zoomed in clearly to Beloved view and a young was showed up.

"Aha! This is Bro. Steve Lord." remarked Beloved.

"For how long has Steve been coming to your fellowship?" asked Jesus.

"About three years Lord." replied Beloved.

"Steve didn't believe in me Jesus until a year ago." remarked Jesus.

"Oh my God! What?" responded Beloved. "Bro. Steve has been a fervent brother in the church for that three years. If he only believed in you Lord just a year ago, what then has he been coming to church for, for the previous two years?" queried Beloved.

"To win the heart of a damsel in your fellowship. He found this damsel and wanted to have carnal relationship with her representing it as a genuine love. But the damsel insisted she would only agree to his request, if he is a Christian. In order to make her believe he is a Christian, he started attending the fellowship, while deep down in his heart he hated me. He was so intentional about her that he didn't give up for two years even as much as the damsel was not forthcoming. But one day, during one of your services, the Holy ghost was moving mightily and invaded his life. He knew something happened to him but didn't know what it was until he got home and had a serious encounter with me—the Lord for eighteen hours. After that encounter he believed me and surrendered his life under my Lordship." explained Jesus.

"Wow! Thank you Lord. Who could have thought there was a member in the fellowship for two years who hated God and deceived the brethren as if he loved God." remarked Beloved.

"There are many like that in my house who don't believe me but do come to my house to pursue their ungodly interest." Jesus added. "Some come to find an argument against me in your teaching and doctrines, some come to occasion a fall for as many brethren as they can, some come to render their service and make profit—those people you pay to do certain things in my house for instance, to play musical instruments, handle sound systems and electrical appliances and so on. Some of them don't believe in me. These people though, fervent in service, are natural men."

"Please Lord have mercy upon them all". Beloved pleaded.

And Jesus replied, "I do have mercy on whom I will. You need to contend in prayers for the veil in their eyes to be removed. For it is the gods of this world who have blinded their eyes that they may not see the light of the glory of God in my face."

"Yes Lord." responded Beloved.

"Finally on a natural man," said Jesus, "Although his spirit is dead to God, it may remain active in other respects. It can be manipulated by evil spirits. Evil spirits can possess the spirit of such a man and use it for their evil works. In this instance, the spirit of a natural man will be stronger than his soul or body and gain dominion over his entire being. For instance, sorceresses and the witches who interact with the spiritual realm but through evil spirit and not through the Holy spirit. That means natural man who is dead to God can yet, be very much alive to Satan by following the evil spirit which has now possessed his spirit."

Beloved nodded his head in understanding.

At that point, Jesus looked into Beloved eyes and said, "The case of the two sisters of your fellowship, who you're burdened with cannot be treated under natural man since they are both regenerated Christians, so it will be treated in the next category."

8 A CARNAL MAN

"What is the next category Lord?" Beloved asked.

The next category is of Christians, those who have passed out of death into life by the imparting of the life of God into their spirits. There are two kinds of Christians—the spiritual Christians and the carnal Christians." replied Jesus.

"And both of them are born of God?" queried Beloved.

"Yes Beloved, they are," Jesus answered. "At new birth, imparting of God's life is not the end of the Christian experience rather, it is the beginning of Christian journey. Although the life of God received is perfect, yet it is just like a child born as a royal crowned prince. No matter how beautiful and excellent the life he is born to live, he is still a baby and will definitely be childish. So also, at the moment of new birth, the life cannot be full grown in a new born Christian, it requires to be nurtured into maturity and that maturity is a stage where the Holy spirit brings such a Christian into complete victory over soul and body. Therefore, a carnal Christian is one who is born anew and has received God's life in him but he is still dominated by flesh instead of dominating the flesh. That means, instead of following the spirit, he still follows the soul and body. As much as it is true that God has provided full salvation in Calvary for the regeneration of sinners and the complete victory for believer over his fallen creation, it is only by constant yielding and obedience to the spirit that this salvation can be fully wrought in the life of a believer. Any believer who fails in this regard will remain a carnal believer sold under sin as he is still under the control of soul and flesh and will be prone to fulfilling the lusts of the flesh and self no matter how many years he's been born again. This was the issue Apostle Paul had with the born again Corinthians in 1 Corinthians chapter 1. He expected them to have grown from babes to maturity but they were still babes for they were carnal showing forth envying, strife and division, which are all works of the flesh that issued from their sinful soul and body as you have read them in Galatians 5."

Beloved sighed while Jesus continued, "Remember that the soul and body still retain their nature, as it is only the spirit that was quickened by the life of God. That means even at regeneration, the soul of a Christian still retains its selfish deeds while his body still retains its fleshy deeds. Thus, salvation comes with a responsibility on believers that having received the Holy spirit in them, they should totally, diligently and constantly yield and obey the spirit and by so doing, they with their soul and body, will become servants to righteousness, for righteousness is the life of God that the Holy spirit leads and guides believers to live, and being slave to righteousness, they shall be free from the sins of the soul and body, and being free from sin, they shall have their fruits unto Holiness and the end for them will be everlasting life (Romans chapter 6). However, a believer who fails to totally, diligently and constantly yield and obey the spirit in this manner, will be at the mercy of the sinful soul and flesh. And no matter how much and how long he disciplines himself or he is disciplined by men, he remains carnal and one day when he will not be able to restrain himself and no one is there to discipline him, he will satisfy that lusts of the flesh and of self.

"Hmm! Lusts of the flesh and self?" Muttered Beloved to himself but Jesus could hear that.

"Yes! Lusts of the flesh and self." responded Jesus. "A carnal believer can either be fleshy—of the body or selfish—of the soul or even both. A fleshy believer is the one who is controlled by his fleshy-body the seat of his senses, while a selfish-soulical believer is one who is controlled by his fleshy-soul, the seats of his emotions, intellects and desires. A believer who is still being controlled by his body-flesh will still commit sin for all that is in the flesh is sin. For they that are after the flesh do mind the things of the flesh and they that are in the flesh cannot please God (Romans 8:5&8). Even if they have genuine desire to do the will of God, so far thy are under the control of the flesh, they will not be able to do it because the flesh lusts against the Spirit, and the Spirit against the flesh: and these are contrary the one to the other: so that ye cannot do the things that ye would (Galatians 5:17). A believer who is of the flesh may for a long time live without sin when there is no occasion or opportunity to sin, but once there's occasion and opportunity, the flesh will take over him and being a slave to the flesh, he will definitely obey his master and commit sins such as Adultery, fornication, uncleanness, lasciviousness, Idolatry, witchcraft, hatred, variance, emulations, wrath, strife, seditions, heresies, envyings, murders, drunkenness, revellings and the likes."

"So, the fact that a Christian has not sin for a long while doesn't mean she's not carnal." Beloved realized.

"Take a look" Jesus beckoned on Beloved. Beloved began to watch some events on the earth cast before him.

The events began with Janet packing away from her lesbian partner, just immediately after she became born again. She moved into her own room apartment and was living alone. Several times, that lust of homosexuality in her flesh arose, but she didn't satisfy it. She thought she was becoming spiritual by not satisfying the urge and was very happy and believed she was free. She was then becoming deep and rooted in the word of God and fervent in the fellowship. She enjoyed the grace of God so much that she was opened to so much revelations. And so she became the vice-president of the fellowship. However, her yielding to the Holy spirit was not constant and total. She was in her room one day having done fasting, studying the scriptures and praying, she set out to watch a movie and the Holy spirit asked her not to watch. Yet she went ahead watching and saw several homosexual scenes in the movie that aroused the urge for such in her. She became uncomfortable with watching the movie but still watched it all through. That reoccurred several times and she wouldn't stop watching. Then the urge to watch movies that display lesbianism was becoming so strong in her and often times she would watch to her satisfaction and she was still doing well in the service of the Lord.

Then Debbie showed up. Debbie was addicted to masturbation before she got born again. And she had to quit leaving alone and moved in with a born again roommate so as not to give an occasion for the act anymore. She really struggled a lot with the addiction. Even though she was living with a roommate, there were times when her roommate wouldn't be around and she would engage in the act again. She believed that as a born again Christian, she should not sin anymore by default, so anytime she fell into masturbation, she would confess Jesus again and again. She might go six to eight months without it but anytime the urge came very strong and there was no hindrance, she would satisfy the urge. That continued until she was given some duties in the fellowship due to her fervency, prayer life and the gifts of the spirit she had. So, she became so busy that she almost didn't have time for herself and her walk in the spirit was irregular. She would yield to the spirit when the desires of the flesh were not too strong to overcome her but when they were, she would easily succumb to the flesh.

Still watching, Beloved saw how Debbie and Janet became very close in the fellowship and how they decided to be staying together believing that they are prayer partners. Their living together was a trouble for Debbie's flesh whenever she saw Janet naked. The urge for lesbianism was getting stronger in her. Yet, she never quit watching lesbian movies whenever her flesh demanded. She just finished watching it one day when Janet came back home and put off her clothes to shower. Then Debbie's urge for homosexuality arose and since flesh has often times have power over her, she couldn't but obey her master—flesh. So, she moved to Janet and began to touch her naked body. Janet was confused at first, then Debbie explained what she was trying to do and how she was addicted to it before. Janet who knew that was wrong and strange couldn't resist as the passion for sexual satisfaction in her own flesh too arose, being a person still struggling with masturbation. They did it and enjoyed it. But after the desires of their flesh has been satisfied, they realized they had just done something against God. They both had a marathon prayer and fasting to plead God for forgiveness. It happened again twice after the first time and it was on the fourth time that they were caught in such an embarrassing and shameful situation.

Beloved watched all that with so much sadness in his heart. "So they both failed to work out their own salvation with fear and trembling." remarked Beloved.

"Now you get it." responded Jesus. "My divine power has given unto them everything pertaining to life and godliness, but these things are in the Holy spirit in their spirit if only they will learn to constantly yield to it. Debbie kept yielding to the flesh by watching those movies, but she thought she would never fulfil the urge for homosexuality that the movies aroused in her. The reason why she didn't fulfill those desires while leaving alone was not because she was free from flesh but because there was no opportunity to fulfill it, as there was no partner in sight. That she can still fulfil one desire of the flesh which is watching those movies means that flesh still has dominion over her. And Janet thought being born again means she was automatically freed from sin, since her flesh has been crucified with me. While it is true that the flesh of a born again Christian has been crucified with me, yet it is a reality that every believer must responsibly align with, not just quote, for them to work in the experience of it. And you align with it by walking in the spirit. That scripture says, 'walk in the spirit, and you shall not fulfill the lust of the flesh' (Galatians 5:16). For it is through the spirit that you can mortify the deeds of the body (Romans 8:13)."

"Lord, how much and how long can a new believer denied the flesh to be totally free from it?" Beloved questioned.

A new believer may not immediately after regeneration begin to walk constantly according to the spirit. Just like a new born baby may not walk immediately after birth. Such a believer may still struggle with flesh for a while just as such a new baby may struggle with walking for a while. But after sometimes, such a believer is expected to have grown from a baby to an adult who can now be intentional and constant with walking and yielding to the spirit. And that's the disappointment Apostle Paul had with the Corinthians, considering how long they have received the new birth he expected them to have grown up and become one with the spirit of God with their souls and bodies, such that they will not show forth works of the flesh anymore. That stage where a believer unites with the spirit of God with his soul and body is a stage where such believer can be free totally from flesh. As his soul and body will now conform to the life of God in his spirit. So a believer is not expected to be a baby for so long, as that will make him subject to the control of his soul and body and ultimately, will hinder God's salvation from realizing its full potential in the believer's life. The flesh has been crucified once with Jesus on the cross, but a believer needs to deny the self everyday of his life. This responsibility is what Debbie and Janet failed to take and that allowed flesh to retain its power over them, despite the number of years they have been born again."

"And you gave them spiritual gifts and graces Lord." remarked Beloved.

"Those are by grace and not by work," replied Jesus. "Sometimes, spiritual gifts are given to help believers in certain areas of their weakness or disadvantages. And at times, to seduce them into alignment. They are never a proof that a man is not carnal. Even the carnal Corinthians lacked no gift (1 Corinthians 1:7)."

"Oh!" Beloved realized. "And what about the second kind of a carnal Christian Lord?"

Jesus answered elaborately, "These are believers who live a soul life and not a spirit life. These believers realize they need to be free from the sin of the mortal body and live a holy and righteous life. But instead of leaning on the Holy spirit for that, they lean on self. They train and discipline their soul to do good, to keep God's commandment and to serve God. That means they rely on their soul life to please God, not mindful that they that are in the flesh cannot please God; for soul life no matter good it does is still carnal. In fact, it is born of the flesh because the soul is of the first Adam-a living soul, which is earthly, natural, physical and ultimately, it is corruption, but the spirit is of the last Adam-a quickening spirit which is spiritual. Therefore soul life is corruption and it cannot inherit the kingdom of God (1 Corinthians 15: 45-50). Accordingly, the scripture also says, 'For he that sows to his flesh shall of the flesh reap corruption; but he that sows to the Spirit shall of the Spirit reap life everlasting' (Galatians 6:8). Therefore the body is fleshy and the soul is fleshy as well, as Apostle Paul described it in his letter to the Ephesians, speaking of their past time without God as a time spent in the lusts of their flesh, fulfilling the desires of the flesh and of the mind which made them by nature the children of wrath (Ephesians 2:3). Similarly, Colossians 2:18 described a fleshy mind as a mind that is vainly puffed up."

Beloved nodded his head severally, he was definitely more enlightened. And Jesus continued, "These believers rely and trust in themselves for keeping commandment of God and as such, they glory in themselves for not committing sin. This is called the boasting of the flesh or confidence in the flesh as against in Christ Jesus even as the scripture says, 'for we are the circumcision, which worship God in the spirit, and rejoice in Christ Jesus, and have no confidence in the flesh' (Philippians 3:3). By glorying or boasting in themselves, they transgress against God for the scripture commands that 'no flesh should glory or boast in the presence of God' (1 Corinthians 1:29), and James condemned all such boasting as evil (James 4:16).

"Oh!" Beloved exclaimed.

"Their error is that they just want to be free from the bad of the flesh and do the good. But in actual fact, both the good and the bad of the flesh is enmity against God; for anyone who lives by the good of the flesh is still under the control of the flesh and later or sooner will do the bad of the flesh because such person is a servant to the flesh. No matter how good, honorable, virtuous, noble and moral the deeds of a soul life, it cannot do the righteousness of God for the only means by which the righteousness of God can be done is through the life of God which is imparted into the believer's spirit, and that's the reason Romans 8:4 states 'that the righteousness of the law might be fulfilled in us, who walk not after the flesh, but after the Spirit'. So unless a believer lives by that spirit, everything he does by the soul life no matter how noble, cannot fulfill the righteousness of God for man's righteousness which a soul life does is like a filthy rags before God (Isaiah 64:6)." Jesus added.

Aha! That's what we call self-righteousness" remarked Beloved.

"You're right" said Jesus. "And do you know what does fleshy—carnal soul life brings to believers?"

"No Lord." replied Beloved.

"First, it brings them absolute loss, for the flesh has no profit, it is the spirit that quickens (John 6:63). Secondly, it brings them condemnation as it is written in Romans 8:1-2, 'there is therefore now no condemnation to them which are in Christ Jesus, who walk not after the flesh, but after the Spirit.' There's no more condemnation for those in Christ Jesus who walk after the spirit because the law of the spirit of life in Christ Jesus has made them free from the law of sin and death. But them who walk after the flesh haven't failed to walk after the spirit, cannot have that law of the spirit of life in Christ Jesus liberate them. So there's still condemnation for them whether they realize it or not. Thirdly, they cannot do that which is good in the eyes of God even though they do that which is good in the eyes of men and even in the eyes of other believers. According to the lamentation of Apostle Paul in Romans 7:18, 'For I know that in me, that is, in my flesh, dwells no good thing: for to will is present with me; but how to perform that which is good I find not'. Fourthly, it brings them into enmity with God because 'a mind governed by the flesh is hostile to God; it does not submit to God's law, nor can it do so' (Romans 8:7 NIV). Also, it brings them into death in this world which is death to the spirit of God as they will not yield to it, and death in eternity, for to be carnally minded is death but to be spiritually minded is life and peace. (Romans 8:6)." Jesus elucidated.

"Aw! Surely, It's not a life at all." observed Beloved.

"No it's not. Because it is only the spirit that giveth life (2 Corinthians 3:6)." responded Jesus. "You have read about Cornelius?"

Beloved replied in the affirmative.

"Cornelius was a man who did all good things commanded by the law with his whole heart but yet it doesn't satisfy God because he was not born of the spirit but of the flesh and that which is born of the flesh is flesh but that which is born of the spirit is spirit. So God brought him in contact with Peter that he might lead him into the experience of new birth and that would enable him through his Holy spirit quickened spirit, to do that which is good, acceptable and perfect will of God." stated Jesus.

Beloved sighed heavily.

"Would you love to see one of your fellowship brethren leaving a soul life?" asked Jesus.

"Yes Lord!" Beloved replied eagerly.

Jesus asked him to take a look on the earth scene again, and Alice popped up. "What? Alice! Alice?" Beloved exclaimed in surprise.

“Yes Alice!" replied Jesus, "Her good, disciplined, religious and righteous life that you all laud and respect so much is self-life, that is self-righteousness. Everything is produced by her soul and not the spirit. And that's why she doesn't believe all that works is by grace, but rather believes they are by her self power and self-determination. So, when she sees or hear of any believer who is not standing right with God, she makes mockery of them for being too weak to work God works. And you would perceive that in the way she reacted to Janet and Debbie issue. She may seem to have burden but not a burden of the spirit. It is merely a zeal in his heart to make people see her doing things for God and in her ignorant mind, to make God consider her for a reward. Most times, the spirit drops things in her mind but she corrupts it by accepting it with her soul life. To raise a personal intercessory prayer for both Janet and Debbie was a burden the spirit dropped in her heart but her-self didn't will that and so she accepted it as an intercessory prayer for the fellowship, and gathered brethren to pray together as that reveal her more. She is like the Galatians who having begun in the spirit sought perfection by the flesh—it is foolishness (Galatians 3:3). If she had done the exact bidding of the spirit, Debbie might not have continued in her iniquity. But for the sake of the righteous believers she gathered for the prayer, my spirit gets involved and begins to direct the prayer according to my will, and puts someone else to the charge of the prayer. And for this cause, Alice is not as passionate with the prayer as she was when she was in charge, doing it her own way.

"Oh my God! Lord have mercy on her" Beloved pleaded.

9 A SPIRITUAL MAN

"Lord! Who then cannot sin?" asked Beloved.

"A spiritual man. A spiritual man cannot sin." answered Jesus.

Seriously curious about that, Beloved questioned further, "Who is a spiritual man Lord?"

And Jesus answered, "A spiritual man is one who constantly and entirely leans on the spirit for his life. He doesn't dwell sometimes on the spirit and other times on the soul or body, he solely dwells on the Holy spirit which dwells in his spirit at all times. Everything about a spiritual man comes from the spirit. His entire being is governed by the Holy spirit which takes him through several spiritual experiences from the dividing of the soul from the spirit to the uniting of his spirit with the Lord. Dividing the outer man(soul and body) from the inner man, and rendering the outer man subject and servant to the inner man is the process the Holy ghost takes a believer through unto spirituality. A spiritual man does not trust himself to please God or do righteousness, he depends solely on the Holy spirit even as the scripture says that 'For we through the Spirit wait for the hope of righteousness by faith' (Galatians 5:5). Spiritual life is maintained only by following the intuition of the spirit always. A spiritual man realizes that in him dwells no good thing and so he relents on the spirit as his only hope to do that which is good, acceptable and perfect will of God. He admits the weakness of his flesh that is, his soul and body and therefore looks to the Holy spirit for strength. It is the office of Jesus to make man regenerated, while it is the office of the Holy spirit to make man spiritual. Therefore, a working relationship with the Holy spirit produces a spiritual man. It is a daily relationship that believers must be intentional, conscious, prayerful and watchful about by denying everything of the soul and body daily and yielding to everything of the Holy spirit in their spirit daily as Apostle Paul mentioned in 1 Corinthians 15:31."

Beloved sighed as Jesus continued, "a spiritual man receives the things of God from the Holy spirit. He inquires and discerns all things by the Holy ghost (1 Corinthians 2:15). That means, a spiritual man will receive of the spirit, consider by the spirit and do by the spirit. He will never at any stage use his self-power or ability. He gives himself constantly to the word of God beholding the glory of God in it, and as he does that he is transfigured by the Holy spirit into the same image of God in Holiness, righteousness and purity. For this cause he will be sinless, for the image of whom he has become is sinless (2 Corinthians 3:18). A spiritual man is a true worshipper as he worships God in his spirit and in truth. He doesn't worship God with a feigned heart, motive or intention, he worships God with a sincere and open heart (John 4:23-24). He has come to know the law of the spirit of life in Christ Jesus, and that makes him free from the law of sin and of death, and the righteousness of the law is fulfilled in him. (Romans 8:1-3). He sets his mind on the things of the spirit every day. He still has the flesh and it's lusts thereof, but he doesn't seek to end the lusts of his flesh by his power rather, through the power of the Holy spirit he habitually put to death—make extinct, deadened the evil deeds prompted by the body (Romans 8:13). By walking in the spirit, a spiritual man cannot fulfill the lust of the flesh (Galatians 5:16)."

"Hmm! Can it be said that a spiritual man is a perfect man?" Beloved inquired.

Jesus smiled and replied, "a spiritual man is a weak man that is made perfect in Christ by the Holy ghost, because it is God that makes perfect for the scripture says, 'Now the God of peace, that brought again from the dead our Lord Jesus, that great shepherd of the sheep, through the blood of the everlasting covenant, make you perfect in every good work to do his will, working in you that which is well pleasing in his sight, through Jesus Christ; to whom be glory for ever and ever. Amen.' (Hebrews 13:20-21). The Holy spirit makes a spiritual man perfect in the Lord in many ways. One of these is through the scriptures as it is written, 'All scripture is given by inspiration of God, and is profitable for doctrine, for reproof, for correction, for instruction in righteousness, that the man of God may be perfect, thoroughly furnished unto all good works (1Timothy 3:16-17). Another way is through ministry gifts as it is written, "And he gave some, Apostles; and some, prophets; and some, evangelists; and some, pastors and teachers; for the perfecting of the saints... (Ephesians 4:12-13). Therefore, a spiritual man admits his weakness and he is strengthened with might by God's Spirit in his inner man. For God's strength is made manifest in weakness as I said in the scripture to Paul that 'My grace is sufficient for thee: for my strength is made perfect in weakness' (2 Corinthians 12:9)."

"Aha!" exclaimed Beloved, as that was revelatory to him.

"Beloved, my will is that you all as believers should become spiritual, for this purpose I died and have you crucified with me, and I rose again and you are risen with me; and as lively stones, you are built up a spiritual house, an holy priesthood, to offer up spiritual sacrifices, acceptable to God by me—Jesus Christ (1 Peter 2:5). My Apostle Paul fully stated this my will in Hebrews 1:1-2 when he said 'Therefore let us go on and get past the elementary stage in the teachings and doctrine of Christ—the Messiah, advancing steadily toward the completeness and perfection that belong to spiritual maturity. Let us not again be laying the foundation of repentance and abandonment of dead works—dead formalism and of the faith by which you turned to God. With teachings about purifying, the laying on of hands, the resurrection from the dead, and eternal judgment and punishment. These are all matters of which you should have been fully aware long, long ago (Amp).' For this purpose, you were sealed with the Holy Spirit as a guarantee and foretaste of the nature of God in you, as you wait in anticipation of full redemption of your corrupt body and soul from their corruption, so that you can acquire the complete possession of the nature of God to the praise of His glory (Ephesians 1:13-14)." Jesus added.

"Help us Lord to live according to your will." Beloved prayed.

"However, being a spiritual man is not an automatic state. If a spiritual man chooses to disobey or ignore the leading of the spirit and follow the flesh, he will bring up fruits and works of the flesh. Therefore, a spiritual man must be intentional and watchful so as not to at any time, turn from the Holy spirit to flesh as that will reduce him to a carnal man." Jesus clarified.

Beloved inquired, "Lord, could there be anyone in the fellowship who is this spiritual?"

Jesus looked at him, smiled and held his hand.

10 WORK OUT YOUR OWN SALVATION

As Jesus held Beloved's hand, Beloved found himself consciously back in his room. It had been a three day journey. And before Beloved could realize it, Jesus had disappeared from the room. Beloved looked so pale as that marked his fifty-two days of staying indoor.

"Thank you Jesus, for giving me the answer. In your mercy, I didn't labour in vain." He said as he stood up. He reached out to a bottle of water, a fruit juice and cereal which he took steadily and at interval within three hours. After that he took a thorough shower and slept till the following day. When he woke up, he was refreshed and then went to his table, took his pen and jotter and wrote down everything about the revelation.

Beloved contacted Julian and Thomas and they came to his house to see him. They were all happy to see again.

"Pastor Beloved, it's almost two months. We were all worried about you" said Thomas.

"Look at you Pastor Beloved, you've lost several pounds." remarked Julian.

Beloved chuckled and replied, 'Thank you brothers, I had to seek the face of God on the latest saddening occurrence in the fellowship."

"Okay, that's good Pastor. Even the brethren were praying vigorously for the fellowship and for you while you were away." said Thomas.

Beloved grinned and appreciated them. "I'm sorry it took this long, while I was praying, Adam and Jesus Christ my Lord came to me."

"What ? You meant you saw Jesus?" asked Julian.

"Yes. He came into this room to answer my cry. He gave me the answer to this sad happenings in the fellowship." Beloved responded.

"What did he say?" both Thomas and Julian chorused.

On that, we are going to have a three day conference. The theme will be 'Work out Your own Salvation' text is Philippians 2:12." responded Pastor Beloved.

He gave the brothers the details, and they went ahead and planned the conference. They made a great publicity through several media outlets all over the city.

In attendance at the conference were both fellowship members and outsiders. Even many who had left the fellowship came for the conference just because Pastor Beloved was the minister. It was a very powerful conference in the city. On the first day, Pastor Beloved taught them on man, on the second day he taught them on salvation and on the last day he taught them on their responsibility in salvation unto spirituality. Believers were coming out in troops to repent of their carnal life after being enlightened on who a carnal Christian is. Many who thought they were doing well in Christ realized that they've been living a soul life all the while and they came out to repent of their self-righteousness including Alice. The conference teachings really came out with the tangible power of the Holy ghost convicting people of righteousness.

Even Janet wept bitterly and realized where she had failed in working out her own salvation with fear and trembling.

The Sunday that followed the conference was declared Holy ghost Sunday. Many were baptized in the Holy ghost and many who have been baptized already were more baptized with hunger and passion for the knowledge and intimacy with the Holy ghost. Pastor Beloved preached on how to know, discern and walk with the Holy spirit. It was such an impactful program for them all.

After the conference, the fellowship members Increased significantly. Many who had left returned and many who were never members of the fellowship joined them. Pastor Beloved got to know about how bad Debbie's depravity had become and he organized a one on one meeting with her, gave her the messages of the conference and prayed with her. Debbie ignored the message for a while but one a particular day, she realized the messages were just occupying memory spaces on her device so she thought of deleting them. However, she changed her mind and decided to listen to those messages before deleting them. Whilst listening to them, she had a turnaround encounter with the Lord and that brought her back to God but she never went back to RSF. Not only that, she became hungry and thirsty to know the person of the Holy spirit and overtime, she entered into an unusual level of oneness with the Holy spirit. She later became a great minister of God who went about Preaching freedom from sexual perversion by the word of her testimony. She was anointed with a powerful and unusual healing anointing that healed people of their spiritual infirmities. Just five years in ministry and over three hundred people have been totally free from their sexual lusts under Minister Debbie's ministry.

Rose of Sharon Fellowship continued having the conference annually and created a class for new believer where they were guided on how to work out their own salvation on their journey to spirituality. Eventually, everyone in the fellowship came into perfect knowledge of the two Adams and how to put off the first Adam which is corrupt according to the deceitful lusts, and put on the second Adam which after God is created in righteousness and true Holiness—Ephesians 4:22-24.

END.

ABOUT THE AUTHOR

ALFRED BETHEL was born in Western Nigeria. He grew up as the son of minister of God-parents who are teachers of the gospel, and he has had several personal encounters with God.

Alfred is not only a believer but also a steward of the manifold grace of God, who by the grace of God has received the spirit of wisdom, insight and revelation in the knowledge of God.

Alfred is a writer who is passionate about sharing and teaching about the things of God and that which God has revealed to him in His son Jesus Christ, confirming and establishing them with the truth, spirit and life of the word of God as contained in the scriptures.

Alfred is also a Christian scriptwriter and a playwright who has written plethora of Holy ghost inspired scripts for church ministrations. Additionally, he has also written over 70 gospel songs as a songwriter.

www.ingramcontent.com/pod-product-compliance
Lightning Source LLC
LaVergne TN
LVHW050344160826
845677LV00014B/3784

* 9 7 9 8 3 5 8 2 1 0 3 7 0 *